ISBN 1-85974-436-2

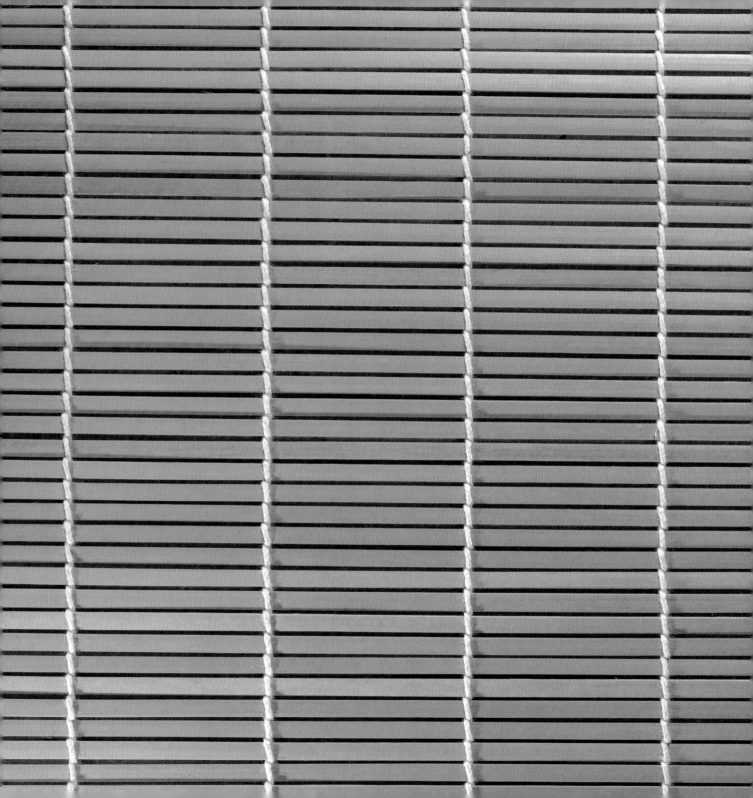

SUSHI

MADE EASY

Sterling Publishing Co., Inc., New York

Library of Congress Cataloging-in-Publication Data Available

10 9 8 7 6 5 4 3 2 1

Published in 2001 by Sterling Publishing Company, Inc.
387 Park Avenue South, New York, N.Y. 10016
Distributed in Canada by Sterling Publishing
c/o Canadian Manda Group, One Atlantic Avenue, Suite 105
Toronto, Ontario, Canada M6K 3E7

Original edition published by New Holland Publishers (UK) Ltd.

DEVELOPED AND DESIGNED BY MICHELE GOMES
TEXT WRITTEN BY NOEL COTTRELL
PHOTOGRAPHY BY DIRK PIETERS
EDITED BY LINDA DE VILLIERS
ILLUSTRATED BY INGRID McGREGOR AND TRACEY KING
SUSHI CRAFTED BY KUMFOO WONG

The utensils and ingredients were supplied by Taste of Japan
The sushi and fish supplied by Willoughby & Co V&A Waterfront Cape Town

Every effort has been made to ensure that all the information in this book is accurate. However, due to differing conditions, tools, and individual skills, the publisher cannot be responsible for any injuries, losses, and other damages which may result from the use of the information in this book.

ISBN 1 85974 436 2

Reproduction by Hirt & Carter Cape (Pty) Ltd
Printed and bound by Times Offset (M) Sdn. Bhd., Malaysia.

SUSHI
MADE EASY

FOR CHLOË
THIS BOOK WAS CONCEIVED WHEN SHE WAS
A GRAIN OF RICE

I WOULD LIKE TO THANK CLINTON FOR ALL OF HIS LOVE AND SUPPORT.
ALSO THANKS TO MY MOM & DAD FOR ALWAYS BELIEVING IN ME
AND BEING THE BEST PARENTS EVER IMAGINABLE
(AND FOR TEACHING ME HOW TO ENJOY FOOD & LIFE),
AND TO HEATHER FOR BEING MY BEST FRIEND AND SUPPORTER.
I LOVE YOU ALL FOREVER.

I WOULD LIKE TO SAY A SPECIAL THANKS TO ALAN SCHAPIRO OF
NEWPORT DELI FOR ALL OF HIS TIME AND KNOWLEDGE. MUCH OF THE
INVALUABLE INFORMATION CAME FROM HIM!
LAST BUT NOT LEAST A HUGE THANKS TO NOEL, MY WRITER,
FOR HIS FABULOUS WORDS AND WONDERFUL BEING.
IT'S BEEN FUN!

SUSHI

MADE EASY

目次

CONTENTS

RAW FISH, SURELY NOT!

THE PATH TO ADDICTION IS A SHORT AND PLEASANT ONE.

FRIENDS TAUNT AND TEASE WHEN YOU'RE NOT INITIALLY A WILLING PARTICIPANT. 'JUST TRY IT, IT'S HARMLESS, AN EXPERIENCE YOU'LL NEVER FORGET.'

YOU START ON THE SOFT STUFF. IN A PUBLIC SETTING. EVERYONE'S DOING IT. THEY SEEM ON A COMMON 'HIGH'. YOU CAN'T SAY NO. SOON YOU'RE ONTO THE HARDER STUFF AND CAN'T IMAGINE ENJOYING AN EVENING OUT WITHOUT IT. YOU MUST HAVE IT. THE SMELL, THE TEXTURE, THE DELICATE CHANGES IN MOOD.

THEN ONE DAY YOU DISCOVER YOUR HABIT IS OUT OF CONTROL, SO YOU CAN NO LONGER AFFORD TO SUSTAIN IT IN A 'SOCIAL' SETTING.

YOU MUST HAVE IT IN THE PRIVACY OF YOUR OWN HOME. AT MIDDAY, IN THE MORNINGS EVEN.

IT IS AT THIS, THE MOST SERIOUS STAGE OF ADDICTION, THAT WE ARE ABLE TO LEND A HAND.

FROM EXPERIMENTING WITH HARMLESS VEGETABLE-FILLED ROLLS, TO THE HOOK OF RAW FISH, TO THE FINAL STAGE – THE SHUNNING OF COOKED FISH – OUR HUMBLE BOOK OFFERS A COMPREHENSIVE GUIDE TO THE ART OF CREATING SUSHI AT HOME.

PENNED FROM THE MOUTHS OF THE VERY PEOPLE WHO GOT YOU HOOKED IN THE FIRST PLACE – THE CHEFS.

ENJOY.

WOODEN BOWL FOR MIXING (HANGIRI)

A wooden rice tub for preparing vinegared rice *(shari)* is ideal. It should be porous enough to absorb the excess moisture of the sushi rice.

FAN (UCHIWA)

A large fan (manual or electric) for quickly cooling the rice – ideal for the chef in a hurry.

RICE PADDLE (SHAMOJI)

A paddle made from bamboo is used for tossing the rice kernels and for serving. Rinse with cold water before using to toss the rice, or the rice will stick to the paddle.

BAMBOO ROLLING MAT (SUDARÈ)

Made from skewer-type bamboo sticks woven together with string, this small mat is used when making rolled sushi. Mats are available in two sizes – for making thick and thin rolls. Choose a tightly woven mat, with string ends on one side. After use, wash in water and dry thoroughly to avoid mold.

CLOTH

A cotton or linen cloth is best as it rinses and drains well. The dry cloth is used for the vinegared rice wrapped in *nori (maki-sushi)*.

KITCHEN CHOPSTICKS (SAIBASHI)

These chopsticks are two to three times longer than ordinary chopsticks and enable you to manipulate all kinds of food with one hand.

WOODEN BOWL FOR MIXING

BAMBOO ROLLING MAT

RICE PADDLE

KITCHEN CHOPSTICKS

CLOTH

COLANDER (ZARU)
Traditionally made of bamboo, although metal or plastic is fine, this is used for washing and draining rice and other ingredients.

CHOPPING BOARD (MANAITA)
Traditionally made of wood, but resin and rubber are just as good.

KNIVES
Serrated stainless steel knives cannot be used to make sushi because they tear instead of cutting clean. A good steel knife and a whetstone to sharpen the blade are important.

CLEAVER
A wide, heavy knife capable of cutting through bone.

VEGETABLE KNIFE
Lighter than a cleaver and with a rectangular blade.

FISH KNIVES
These long and slender knives are available with either pointed or blunt-tipped blades and are used for cutting fish into perfect cubes and slices. Sushi chefs keep a folded wet cloth on hand to wipe the blades of their knives while they work.

BOWL FOR VINEGAR

BOWL FOR SOY SAUCE

CLEAVER

VEGETABLE KNIFE

SOUP SPOON

FISH KNIFE

MAKING YOUR OWN PICKLED GINGER (GARI)

To make sweet and sour pickled ginger (GARI), follow these five easy steps.

1. Pare the ginger and cut into thin slices along the fibers.
2. Spread onto a chopping board and sprinkle with a little salt.
Let stand for 20 to 30 minutes until soft.

3. Pour 125 ml (¾ cup) vinegar into a small pot,
add 30 ml (2 tbsp) sugar and 60 ml (4 tbsp) water and bring to a boil.
Let cool. Add two drops of red food coloring
to give the ginger a pinkish tinge.
4. Blanch the ginger in hot water, transfer to a colander and drain.
Cool by fanning.

5. Soak the ginger in the sweet vinegar (su) for about a day, until well
seasoned. After use, gari should be kept in the fridge to
maintain its freshness.

THE MAIN INGREDIENTS

Although all seven of these ingredients appear in the Glossary, the important role each plays in the successful outcome of your sushi cannot be overstated. What follows is a closer look at sushi's half-dozen-plus key players.

RICE VINEGAR (SU)

Only the highest quality rice vinegar is suitable for sushi. It has a gentle tartness and leaves a pleasant aftertaste, and can be bought at most Asian food stores (*Mitsukan* Vinegar is Japan's largest manufacturer). Sugar is often added to the vinegar to prevent the tartness coming through too strongly. When mixing your vinegar with your rice, be careful to follow the instructions as too much vinegar can overwhelm the taste of the fish and ruin your whole meal.

SOY SAUCE (MURASAKI)

Shoyu, as it's commonly called, is essential to traditional Japanese food. It masks the rawness of fresh, uncooked fish and harmonizes with other ingredients such as *nori* (seaweed). Without the slightly salty taste of soy sauce, *nigiri-sushi* might never have achieved the popularity it enjoys today. For those who enjoy the healthy side of sushi, you'll be glad to know soy sauce is on Weight Watchers' list of recommended foods. A lighter soy sauce is also available for those who aren't keen on too much salt. Both varieties are available at most supermarkets and Asian food stores *(Kikkoman* is one of the world's largest manufacturers). Once you've opened your soy sauce, it should be stored in a cool, dark place or refrigerated.

PICKLED GINGER (GARI)

In addition to being a fine mouth freshener, pickled root ginger has antibacterial qualities. The most common *gari* is of the packaged, imported variety, which you'll find at most Asian food stores. For the more adventurous, you can try pickling the ginger yourself (see recipe opposite).

HORSERADISH (WASABI)

Grown only in Japan, *wasabi* horseradish (from the plant *Wasabia japonica*) is a nose-tingling refreshing pulp. The finer the root is ground, the better the *wasabi*. *Wasabi* stimulates the secretion of saliva and digestive juices, sharpening the appetite. Fresh *wasabi* is understandably expensive and is therefore sold in powdered form and as a paste at Asian food stores.

THE MAIN INGREDIENTS

SEAWEED (NORI)

Nori was first cultivated in Tokyo Bay in the seventeenth century. It has a high nutritional value because of its protein, mineral salt, and extremely high vitamin content. After the seaweed is harvested it is washed in fresh water, dried on large frames, cut into sheets, and lightly roasted. The best quality *nori* is black. Since black *nori* is expensive, a cheaper green colored variety is also on the market. A sheet of *nori* is approximately 20 x 22 cm (8 x 9 in). After opening, it should be stored in an airtight container. *Nori* is available in packets from Asian food stores.

FISH

Possibly the most important ingredient in sushi – up there with rice. The one thing to remember is that the fish must be 100 per cent fresh. For sushi you can use any fish except the soft white variety, as this has bacteria that grow rapidly and become toxic. Interestingly, certain fish taste better in certain seasons. When buying your fish, be sure to ask where it was caught, when it was caught, and if it has been frozen. If you're going to eat raw fish, it's best to eat it the day it was caught.

RICE (GOHANMONO)

Most people like to eat newly harvested rice, but for sushi the grains need to have aged a while. Sushi chefs who know their rice have their rice dealers mix grains of different stages of maturity and from various regions to meet their specific requirements. Interestingly, again for the health nuts, rice has only 420 kilojoules (100 calories) per 100 grams (3½ oz). You can get short grain rice suitable for sushi at most Asian food stores.

RICE

If spending 40 minutes in the kitchen perspiring over your weekly roast is much more than a labor of love, contemplate an entire year washing dishes, before being given the honor of another year – cooking rice: the lot of a professional sushi chef, before moving on to things fishier.

Let us not underestimate the importance of rice in Japanese cuisine.

The Japanese variety of rice is known as 'Japonica'. It's short grain, which means the individual grains are round and sticky when cooled (extremely sticky, keep a hand towel nearby). Long grain Indian rice isn't right for sushi because it's too dry and therefore retains too much water.

GETTING THE RICE JUST RIGHT

INGREDIENTS

Serves approximately four (depends entirely on the dish you use it for).

460 g (1 lb) short-grain rice

750 ml (2½ cups) water

VINEGAR MIXTURE

75 ml (5 tbsp) rice vinegar

15 ml (1 tbsp) mirin

45 ml (3 tbsp) sugar

30 ml (2 tbsp) salt

METHOD

Wash the rice until the water runs clear.

Drain for 1 hour, then place the rice in a pot with a tight fitting lid and add the water. Bring to a boil, reduce heat, and simmer for a further 5 minutes.

Lower the heat and steam for 12 to 15 minutes. Remove from heat.

Remove the lid and cover the pot with a tea towel. Let stand for 15 minutes.

While the rice is cooking, combine the vinegar mixture ingredients in a saucepan and heat gently until the sugar dissolves, stirring constantly. Remove the mixture from the heat and cool.

Spread the rice evenly over the base of a shallow, wooden bowl. Run a spatula through the rice to gently separate the grains and slowly add the vinegar mixture at the same time. The rice shouldn't be too moist.

Fan the rice until it reaches room temperature. Keep the rice in the wooden bowl, covered with a clean cloth, until ready to use.

Remember: Although it may take a year to perfect, sushi rice only lasts one day, and should never be kept and served again at a later stage.

F I S H

It's been said before, but fresh fish is the key to great sushi. Basically, if it smells like fish, it's not fresh. When buying your fish make sure it looks, feels, and smells fresh.

So, you're still not too sure if your fish is fresh? Well stare it in the eye – is the eye full, round, and clear, not cloudy? Look under the gill – is it red, not brown? Was it caught today? Has it been frozen? Is the flesh firm, does it spring back if you press it lightly? Okay, your fish is fresh. A tip for the chef in a hurry – if you're buying part of a big fish (a tuna, for example), tell the person cutting your piece that it's for sushi. Ask the same person to debone and fillet the fish for you (making sure the pin bones are removed). Once you've got it home, wrap it in plastic wrap and cover it in crushed ice, top and bottom, in a container and refrigerate. The container should have holes in the bottom, so that the water can drain away as the ice melts.

Now to the cutting. To demonstrate how to cut fish for sushi, we're using tuna *(maguro)* as our example. The method for cutting other fillets is similar. To prepare *maguro,* first the head and tail are removed. Then the flesh is cut from the spine to make two large boneless fillets. These two fillets are cut lengthwise into back (upper) and belly (lower) blocks, which are roughly triangular in cross section. Each of these blocks is called *chó.* A shop will usually purchase one or two *chó* each day. The section of the belly block closest to the body cavity is the fatty *ótoro.* It is expensive. Flesh somewhat less fatty than this *(chútoro)* comes from the belly block near the tail and the back block. The flesh around the spine is lean and red; this is called *akami.* The red flesh near the tail is the least expensive.

So, now you have a sizeable block of fish on your chopping board, you have your fish knife in your hand, a small bowl of rice vinegar (to dip your knife into before cutting anything), and a folded wet cloth nearby (to wipe the blade, remember).
Always remember to cut across the grain.
Cutting fish into slices of uniform size and thickness appropriate for *nigiri-sushi* topping takes skill, which you'll pick up with practice.
So, get practicing.

C U T T I N G   F I S H

To demonstrate how to cut fish topping for sushi, we're using a healthy block of tuna *(maguro)*.

1. Place the tuna on a cutting board and measure the length by laying your hand on the block of tuna – four fingers is just right. Cut this amount off the block of fish.

2. Turn the cut-off block by 90 degrees.

3. Measure off 15 mm (about ⅝ in) from the left side and using a sharp fish knife, slice diagonally downward to the bottom corner, to make a triangular piece of fish.

4. Place this triangular piece cut-side down, and position the knife blade in the middle of the right side of the triangle. Cut about two-thirds of the way through the piece, then use the knife to unfold the piece. This piece of fish is placed bottom-side down on the rice to form the topping (when making *nigiri-sushi).*

5. Continue to cut off slices by measuring off 8 mm (about ⅓ in) along the top and slicing at an angle to form pieces of uniform thickness. The last piece on the right will also be triangular in cross section and must be cut in the same way as the first triangular piece.

If the fish has slanted streaks, put the knife at right angles to the streaks, so that the streaks become short.
Run the knife diagonally downward, then straighten the knife so that it forms a 90 degree angle with the cutting board, cut through and voilà – you have a slice of raw fish.

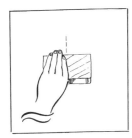  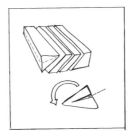 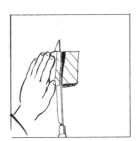

FISH AND SHELLFISH

Soft, white fish is not suitable for sushi because it has bacteria that grow in the flesh of the fish, immediately after the fish has been caught. You can very easily get food poisioning from eating soft white fish raw.

These sushi toppings should be available from your local fishmonger and can be eaten raw. Remember to ask on what days and times the freshest fish is available.

ABALONE (raw)

ARK SHELI (raw)

CLAM (raw)

CONGER EEL (cooked)

CRAB (cooked)

FLATFISH (raw)

MACKEREL (marinated raw)

OCTOPUS (cooked)

ROE (raw or salted)

SALMON (salted, although

can be enjoyed raw)

SEA BASS (raw)

SEA BREAM (raw)

SEA URCHIN (raw or salted)

SHRIMP OR PRAWN (mostly cooked)

SQUID (raw or cooked)

TUNA (raw)

YELLOWTAIL (HAMACHI)

TUNA (MAGURO)

EEL (UNAGI)

SALMON (SAKE)

SURF CLAM (BAKAGAI)

PRAWN (EBI)

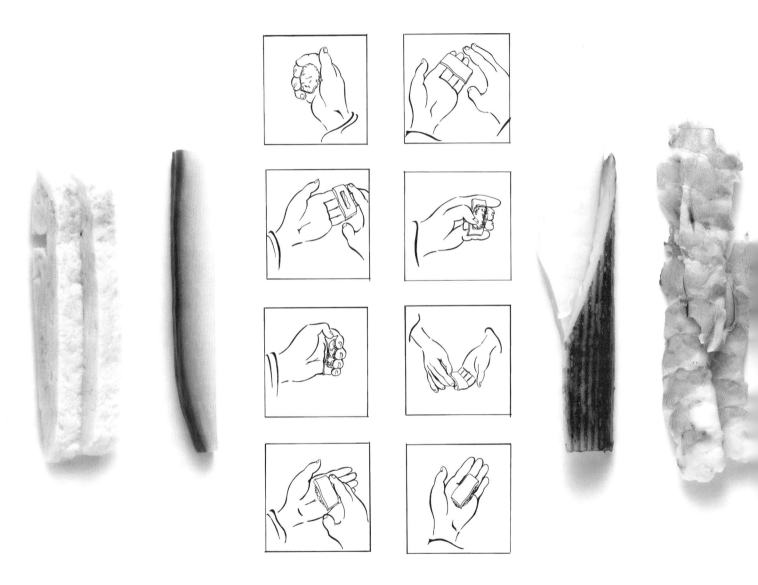

NIGIRI-SUSHI

HOW TO MAKE NIGIRI-SUSHI

Okay, so you've got a bowl of well-cooled rice and raw fish neatly cut into perfect slices. Now to combine the two.

THE PROFESSIONAL 10-STEP METHOD

1. Shape about 30 ml (2 tbsp) vinegared rice *(shari)* into balls the size of a ping-pong ball.

2. Open your left hand and place your piece of raw fish (or whatever other topping you choose) over your fingers just above your palm.

3. Place a small amount of *wasabi* on the fish.

4. Place the rice ball on top of the slice of fish.

5. Gently close your left hand, pressing the rice ball with the ball of the palm.

6. Flip the rice and fish over carefully so that the fish is on the top.

7. Press in the side edges of the *nigiri-sushi* with the thumb and index finger of your right hand.

8. Use your index finger to press down on the surface of the fish.

9. Turn the *nigiri* portion clockwise on your hand.

10. Press lightly once or twice on the ends. Your *nigiri* is ready to serve.

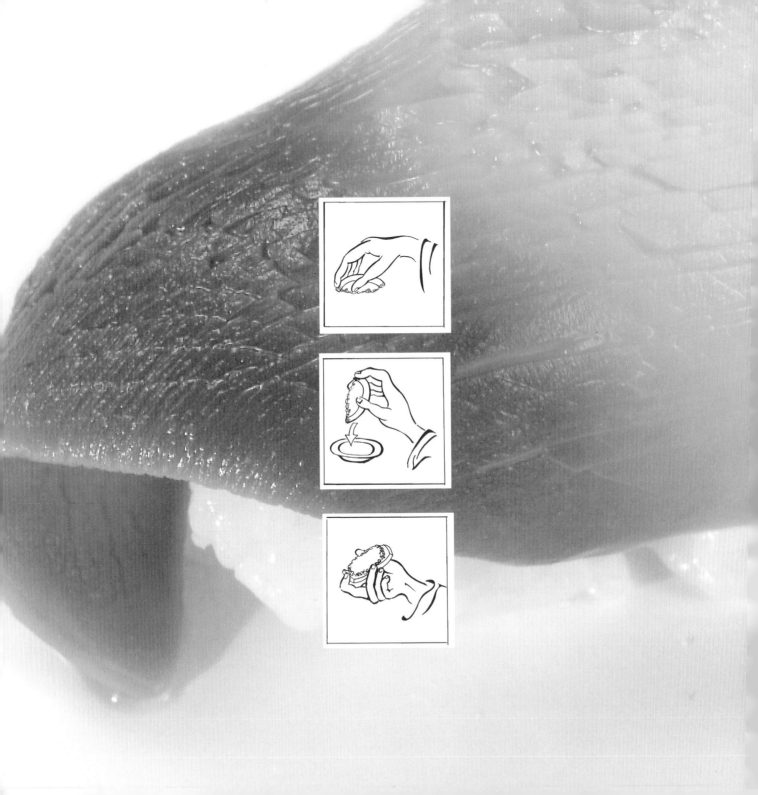

IDEAS FOR TOPPINGS (TANÉ)

Besides the *tané* shown below, other *tané* such as scallops, abalone, octopus, red snapper, clams, grilled seasoned eel, avocado, and rolled egg can also be used.

YELLOWTAIL (HAMACHI)   SALMON (SAKE)   TUNA (MAGURO)

SURF CLAM (BAKAGAI)   FLOUNDER (HIRAME)   PRAWN (EBI)

HOW TO EAT YOUR NIGIRI-SUSHI

To enjoy your *nigiri-sushi*, place some soy sauce (*shoyu*) in a small sauce bowl, pick up the *nigiri-sushi* with your thumb and middle fingers and rest your index finger on the end of the topping. Turn it over carefully so that the topping is on the underside. Now, dip the topping into the soy sauce. You should never place your entire piece of *nigiri-sushi* rice-first into the soy sauce – it's the equivalent of smothering your steak in ketchup – and the rice will disintegrate.

PRAWN (SHRIMP) SUSHI

Not much tops prawn or shrimp as a topping for *nigiri-sushi*.

The Japanese consider fresh raw prawn to be one of the greatest delicacies. Few prawns, however, whether fresh or frozen, are of a high enough quality to be served raw. *Ebi* (cooked prawn) is actually a jumbo shrimp. Your *ebi* must be nicely colored, well shaped, and opened flat to embrace the finger of sushi rice. Here's how to boil them to perfection.

INGREDIENTS

8 raw shrimp or prawns, heads removed

15 ml (1 tbsp) Japanese rice wine *(saké)*

5 ml (1 tsp) salt

dash of rice vinegar *(su)*

METHOD

Clean the prawns by removing any black veins but keeping the tails intact. Spear the prawns with bamboo skewers or toothpicks on the leg side of each shrimp (to prevent curling). The skewer should not pierce the flesh. Cover the bottom of a saucepan with water and bring to a boil. Place the prawns, *saké*, and salt in the water and simmer for 2 minutes. Remove to ice water and chill. When completely chilled, remove the skewers.

Shell the prawns by trimming off the small triangular segments of shell above the tail using the point of a knife, but still leaving the rest of the tail intact. Butterfly the prawns carefully by making an incision along the leg side of the prawn, then deepen the incision so that the prawn can be opened and flattened. Do not cut all the way through the flesh. Sprinkle with rice vinegar. Refrigerate until needed.

HOW TO MAKE PRAWN NIGIRI-SUSHI

METHOD

Shape about 20 g (¼ cup) of sushi rice into a ball with your right hand. Beginners may want to make several rice balls in advance.

Place the butterflied prawn topping on the flattened fingers of your left hand. Hold the rice ball in your right palm and, using the tip of your index finger, place a smear of *wasabi* down the center of the prawn.

Put the ball of rice on the topping and press the top of the rice lightly with your left thumb so that the center does not become too compact. Lightly press the rice on all sides, following the shape of the prawn.

Flip the *nigiri-sushi* over so that the prawn is on top and lightly press the rice on all sides again.

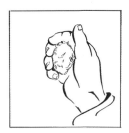  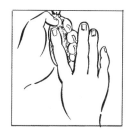 

HOW TO MAKE SUSHI ROLLS (MAKI)

Rolling sushi takes practice. It looks simple enough, but it's not. Sometimes the filling is off center, the rice isn't firm enough or you've left too much seaweed *(nori)* on the edges. Have patience, it'll come.

SLENDER ROLLS (HOSOMAKI)

Hosomaki is a slender, rolled sushi, boasting one to three ingredients instead of the assortment found in the larger *futomaki*. Only half a sheet of nori is used to make *Hosomaki*. You should get six bite-size rounds out of a *Hosomaki*.

INGREDIENTS

500 g (1 lb) vinegared rice *(shari)*

5 sheets seaweed *(nori)*

rice vinegar *(su)*

wasabi

your choice of fillings – tuna *(maguro),* daikon, omelette, crab, cucumber, carrot, etc.

METHOD

Prepare the vinegared rice and place to one side. Cool the rice to room temperature – if it's too cold, it won't stick together well. Cut a sheet of seaweed crosswise into two.

Place one half of the seaweed crosswise and shiny-side down on the surface of the bamboo rolling mat *(sudarè)*. The rolling mat must be dry and placed on a dry chopping board. Moisten your hands in vinegared water *(tezu)* and make a ball out of half a cup of prepared vinegared rice. Place this ball on the seaweed and spread it out carefully. Spread it gently, don't push it down onto the seaweed. Keep about 12 mm (½ in) free of rice on the far end of the *nori* (to seal the roll).

Place a dab of *wasabi* on your index finger and run your finger along the rice, from left to right, in a straight line. This line should be at the end closest to you (so that the filling remains central). Place the fillings for your roll on top of the *wasabi,* and wet the exposed strip of *nori* (not covered with rice) with rice vinegar.

Lift the front of the bamboo mat closest to you. Roll the *hosomaki* by pressing the *sudarè* down firmly on the *nori*. The *nori* will stick to itself when the roll is complete. Shape the ends of the roll so that no rice will fall out and then let the roll rest for a minute or two. Moisten a sharp knife with vinegared water before cutting the roll into four or six neat pieces.

HOW TO MAKE FUTOMAKI

THICK ROLLS (FUTOMAKI)

Thick sushi rolls, filled with colorful ingredients, are perfect for showing off to your dinner guests. *Futomaki* often combines 'cooked' and raw ingredients.

METHOD

1. Place half a sheet of seaweed *(nori)*, shiny-side down, on a bamboo rolling mat. Add a quarter of a sheet by pasting the edges together with crushed rice grains.

2. Leaving about 10 mm (⅜ in) free on the right-hand side of the *nori*, spread an even layer of vinegared rice – about 10 mm (⅜ in) deep – over the rest of the seaweed.

3. Crush rice grains onto the two right-hand corners of the *nori*.

4. Turn the whole sheet by 90 degrees. Now lay the filling for your roll lengthways. Bands of tuna, *kampyó, oboro*, bamboo shoots, cucumber, omelette, and mushroom are a great combination.

5. Rolling the *futomaki* is a delicate procedure. Starting with the edge closest to you, slowly roll up the *nori* in the mat, holding the rows of ingredients in place with your fingertips. Now, join and fasten the corners that were pasted with crushed rice.

6. Press on your bamboo mat to adjust the shape of the roll, so that it's slightly oval. Cut the roll in half and then slice each half into four equal parts. To ensure you cut cleanly, wet your knife in rice vinegar and wipe the blade after each slice.

SUSHI ROLLS (MAKI)

Here are some combinations of ingredients that can be used in sushi rolls. Get creative and try any combinations to find out what really tickles your fancy.

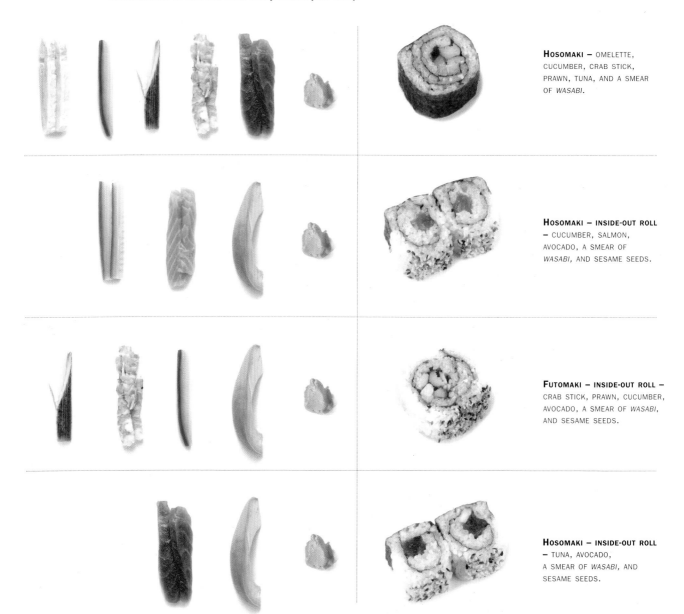

HOSOMAKI – OMELETTE, CUCUMBER, CRAB STICK, PRAWN, TUNA, AND A SMEAR OF *WASABI*.

HOSOMAKI – INSIDE-OUT ROLL – CUCUMBER, SALMON, AVOCADO, A SMEAR OF *WASABI*, AND SESAME SEEDS.

FUTOMAKI – INSIDE-OUT ROLL – CRAB STICK, PRAWN, CUCUMBER, AVOCADO, A SMEAR OF *WASABI*, AND SESAME SEEDS.

HOSOMAKI – INSIDE-OUT ROLL – TUNA, AVOCADO, A SMEAR OF *WASABI*, AND SESAME SEEDS.

SUSHI ROLLS (MAKI)

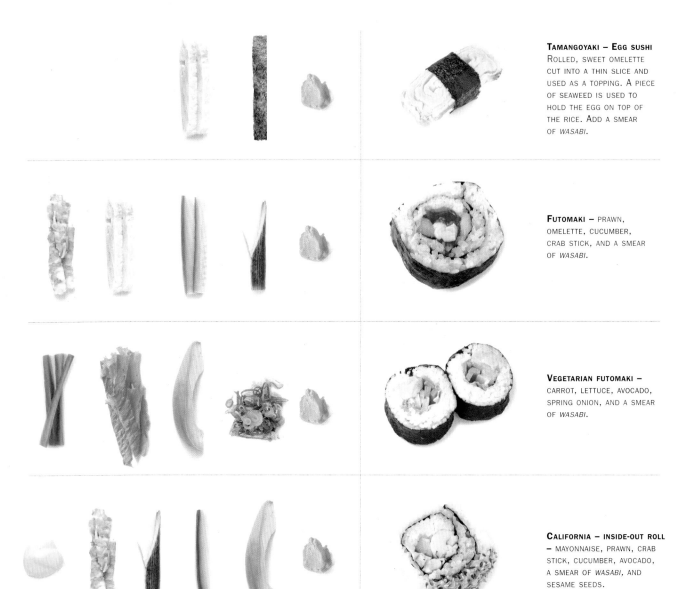

TAMANGOYAKI – EGG SUSHI
ROLLED, SWEET OMELETTE CUT INTO A THIN SLICE AND USED AS A TOPPING. A PIECE OF SEAWEED IS USED TO HOLD THE EGG ON TOP OF THE RICE. ADD A SMEAR OF *WASABI*.

FUTOMAKI – PRAWN, OMELETTE, CUCUMBER, CRAB STICK, AND A SMEAR OF *WASABI*.

VEGETARIAN FUTOMAKI – CARROT, LETTUCE, AVOCADO, SPRING ONION, AND A SMEAR OF *WASABI*.

CALIFORNIA – INSIDE-OUT ROLL – MAYONNAISE, PRAWN, CRAB STICK, CUCUMBER, AVOCADO, A SMEAR OF *WASABI*, AND SESAME SEEDS.

SUSHI ROLLS (MAKI)

TEKKAMAKI – TUNA AND A SMEAR OF *WASABI*.

KAPPAMAKI – CUCUMBER AND A SMEAR OF *WASABI*.

FUTOMAKI – CARROT, LETTUCE, AVOCADO, SALMON ROE, SPRING ONION, AND A SMEAR OF *WASABI*.

HOSOMAKI – CUCUMBER, PICKLED PLUM, AND A SMEAR OF *WASABI*.

SUSHI ROLLS (MAKI)

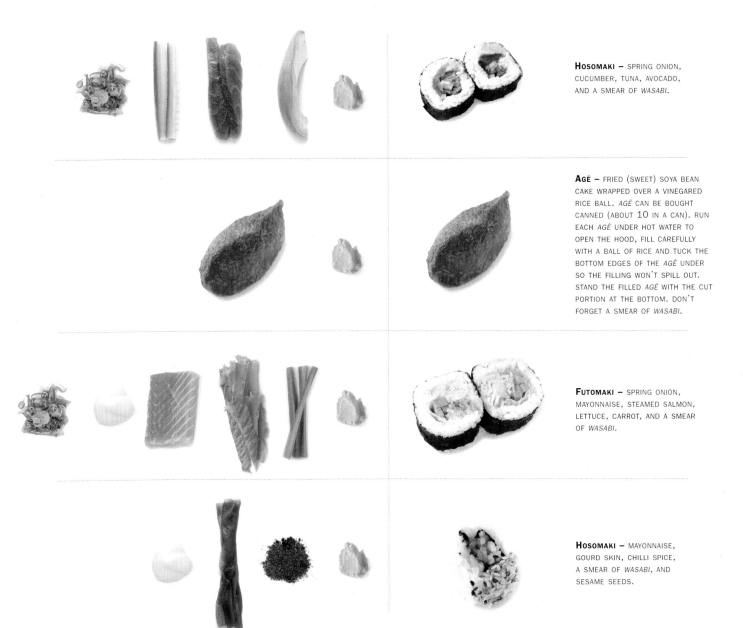

HOSOMAKI – SPRING ONION, CUCUMBER, TUNA, AVOCADO, AND A SMEAR OF *WASABI*.

AGÉ – FRIED (SWEET) SOYA BEAN CAKE WRAPPED OVER A VINEGARED RICE BALL. *AGÉ* CAN BE BOUGHT CANNED (ABOUT 10 IN A CAN). RUN EACH *AGÉ* UNDER HOT WATER TO OPEN THE HOOD, FILL CAREFULLY WITH A BALL OF RICE AND TUCK THE BOTTOM EDGES OF THE *AGÉ* UNDER SO THE FILLING WON'T SPILL OUT. STAND THE FILLED *AGÉ* WITH THE CUT PORTION AT THE BOTTOM. DON'T FORGET A SMEAR OF *WASABI*.

FUTOMAKI – SPRING ONION, MAYONNAISE, STEAMED SALMON, LETTUCE, CARROT, AND A SMEAR OF *WASABI*.

HOSOMAKI – MAYONNAISE, GOURD SKIN, CHILLI SPICE, A SMEAR OF *WASABI*, AND SESAME SEEDS.

BATTLESHIP WRAP (GUNKANMAKI)

To make one roll, mould 25 g (¾ cup) of vinegared rice into a small patty and wrap the rice in a small sheet of *nori* (cut to size). The seaweed should protrude a little above the level of the rice. Dab the top of the rice with *wasabi* before filling the roll with your favorite filling.

Salmon roe, sea urchin roe, cod roe, herring roe, salted crabs eggs *(kani-ko),* shrimp eggs, flying fish, smelt as well as squid, and *kombu* preserved in saké, and soy sauce *(matsumae-zuke)* make great toppings for *gunkanmaki.*

SHRIMP EGGS (UNI)   COD ROE (TARAKO)   SALMON ROE (IKURA)

INSIDE-OUT ROLLS

INSIDE-OUT ROLLS (YUKIWA-MAKI)

To really impress your friends, experiment with inside-out rolls, where the rice lands up on the outside of the seaweed. They are tricky and definitely take practice. You can fill inside-out rolls with any ingredients you choose.

METHOD

1. Cut pickled Daikon radish *(takuan)* and thick omelette into thin slices, and cucumber into thin sticks.

2. Cover your rolling mat with plastic wrap (so the rice won't stick to it). Lay one sheet of *nori* lengthways on the mat and spread 300 g (1¼ cup) of sushi rice over the entire sheet.

3. Sprinkle 30 ml (2 tbsp) toasted white sesame seeds over the rice.

4. Turn the rice-covered *nori* sheet upside-down onto the mat covered in plastic wrap. The rice is now face-down on the plastic wrapped mat. Starting at the end nearest you, place the filling (Daikon radish, omelette and cucumber) on top of the *nori*.

5. Roll the *maki*, starting with the edge nearest you.

6. Use the rolling mat to shape your inside-out roll (as shown below).

7. Remove from the mat and plastic, and cut into neat slices. You should get six servings out of one roll.

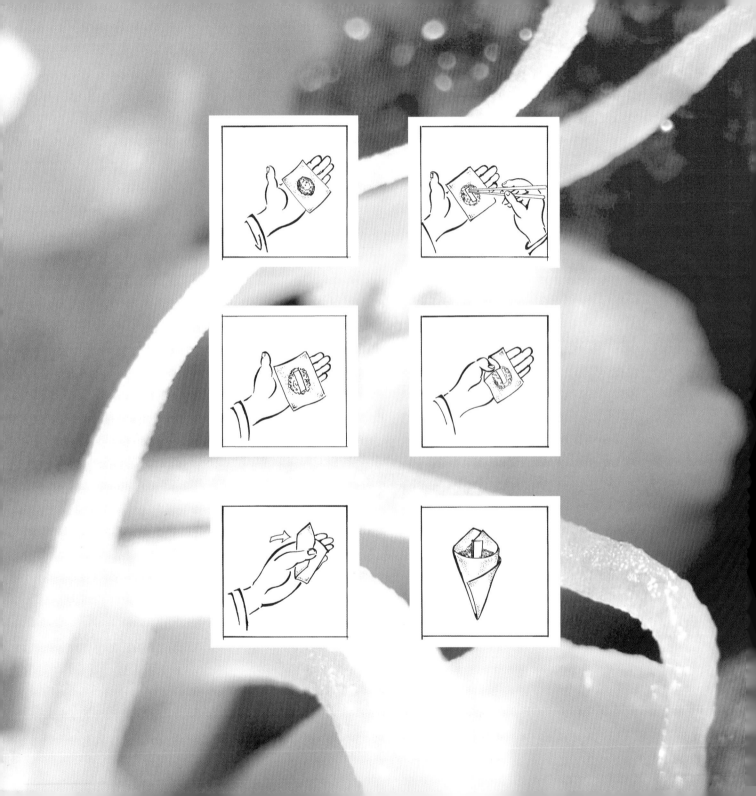

HAND ROLLS

HAND ROLLS (TEMAKI-SUSHI)

Make sure none of your guests go hungry by adding a couple of substantial hand rolls to any platter of sushi or assortment of *maki*. Salmon hand rolls are a big favorite.

METHOD

1. To make ten pieces of *temaki-sushi*, prepare ten ping-pong sized balls of vinegared rice *(shari)*.

2. Place a quarter sheet of *nori* in your open left palm. Put a ball of *shari* in the center of the *nori*.

3. Apply a dab of *wasabi,* using the tip of a chopstick or a small spatula.

4. Next, use chopsticks to place the filling *(néta)* on top of the rice ball and *wasabi*. Great fillings include raw fish, egg, and vegetables.

5. With the left thumb, fold the *nori* over to stick onto the rice. Use a gentle rolling motion of the thumb and fingers to roll the *temaki-sushi* so that the original fold lands up at the bottom of your palm (see opposite).

If the filling, such as salmon roe or sea urchin roe is loose, make the hand roll more cone-shaped. Again remember, practice makes perfect.

1. Place a half sheet of *nori* diagonally on the palm of your left hand.

2. Place the ball of rice on the far left-hand side of the *nori*, add a dash of *wasabi,* and position your choice of filling on the rice. Fold the near corner over so it's a little below the center of the seaweed. Then, slowly close your fingers, to form a cone.

CALIFORNIA HAND ROLL

CALIFORNIA HAND ROLL

Invented on America's West Coast, 'California Rolls' call for fillings of ripe avocado and crab. The oil content and smooth texture of the avocado is similar to tuna *(maguro)*. California Rolls are enjoyed as normal rolls *(maki)* or hand rolls.

METHOD

1. Toast a *nori* sheet and cut it into quarters. Place a quarter sheet of *nori* in your hand.

2. Place a ping-pong sized ball of vinegared rice *(shari)* in the center of the *nori*.

3. Top with a slice of avocado and crab leg (imitation crab – *kani no kamaboko* – is fine) and sprinkle the contents with toasted white sesame seeds.

4. Roll the hand roll into a cone shape.

Another interesting way to enjoy avocado is to sprinkle a piece with lemon juice and place it on a regular *nigiri-sushi*. Shrimp and scallops also taste great with avocado.

ROLLED SWEET OMELETTE

ROLLED SWEET OMELETTE (TAMAGO YAKI)

Rolled omelette can be served as a side dish with sushi.

INGREDIENTS

4 eggs

dash of salt

15 ml (1 tbsp) water

30 ml (2 tbsp) sugar

10 ml (2 tsp) soy sauce *(shoyu)*

45 ml (3 tbsp) *saké* or dry white wine

vegetable oil for cooking

ROLLED SWEET OMELETTE

METHOD

Beat the eggs in a bowl, and add a pinch of salt. Add water to the egg mixture and beat until fluffy. In a small bowl, mix the sugar with the soy sauce and *saké* or wine, and lightly stir into the eggs. Heat a square frying pan over medium heat. Oil the pan lightly (a small piece of cheesecloth is useful to oil the pan), pour in a third of the egg mixture to cover the entire pan. Cook over medium heat. Before the surface begins to dry, roll the egg mixture towards you. Now, move the rolled egg away from you to the far end of the pan. Oil the emptied space. Tilt the pan, adding another third of the mixture under the rolled egg – you can lift it with chopsticks. Continue to fry the mixture. Now, roll the omelette away from you again. Oil the front half of the pan once more. Add the balance of the egg mixture – be sure to pour it under the rolled omelette again. Just before the mixture dries, roll the rest into the already-quite-fat omelette. Slide the roll so that its final join is underneath and cook for 10 seconds.

Now, slide the roll out on to a bamboo mat and roll up tightly. Press it neatly into a rectangular shape and set aside until cool. Slice the cold omelette roll into 25 mm (1 in) thick pieces. Rolled omelette is best enjoyed with *shiso, gari,* and of course, soy sauce *(shoyu)*.

SOUPS

The entire category of Japanese soups is known as *shirumono* and includes both clear and 'thick' soups. Clear soups (*suimono* – literally means 'something to drink') can be served as a 'first course' or can be served mid-way through a meal to clear the palate, in much the same way sorbet is served in sophisticated French cuisine. The Japanese believe good, clear soup is impressive in its purity and restraint and often makes a meal. It's these soups that we'll concentrate on.

Suimono is served by artistically arranging two or three solid ingredients in a bowl, before pouring in a hot clear broth (carefully, so as not to disturb the design) and placing a lid on the bowl to keep it warm. When served, the lid is whipped off the bowl and in a flourish of steam, the design of the floating solid ingredients is revealed.

BASIC CLEAR JAPANESE SOUP (SUIMONO)

While these recipes are simple, it's the presentation that'll take some mastering. Use covered lacquered Japanese bowls if you have them as they retain the heat of the soup best.

BASIC STOCK (DASHI)

Japanese clear soups have no fat, and good stock is crystal clear. The kelp *(kombu)* and bonito fish flakes *(katsuo bushi)* combine to give *suimono* its characteristic sweetness.

METHOD

Fill a saucepan with 1 liter (2½ cups) cold water. Add a 20 cm (8 in) square piece of dried *dashi kombu* (kelp for stock). When the water comes to the boil, remove the *kombu*. Add 30 g (2 tbsp) dried bonito fish flakes *(katsuo)* and immediately remove the saucepan from the heat source. The fish flakes will sink to the bottom of the pan. Strain in a colander lined with cheesecloth. Season with 5 ml (1 tsp) salt, a dash of Japanese rice wine *(saké)*, and a few drops of soy sauce *(shoyu)*. Taste as you add the seasoning to keep the flavor light and delicate.

Tips: If this stock preparation is cooked too long, the *kombu* causes the *dashi* to become cloudy and bitter. You can use instant *dashi* powder or chicken broth – but chances are with the chicken broth, you won't get the same 'Japanese' taste.

CLEAR SOUP WITH SHRIMP

INGREDIENTS

4 medium-size shrimp, shelled but with tails left intact and veins removed

cornstarch

1 fresh string bean, sliced thinly on the diagonal (or use another vegetable such as a carrot)

1 liter (2½ cups) soup base *(dashi)*

salt, *saké*, and a dash of *shoyu*

4 sprigs Japanese pepper plant *(sansho kinomé)* or watercress

METHOD

Lightly salt the raw shrimp, dip in cornstarch and parboil for 2 minutes in boiling water. Boil the string bean or carrot for 1 minute. Heat the soup base. Taste, and if necessary, flavor lightly with salt and *saké*. Add soy sauce *(shoyu)* at the very end, if it needs it.

Put one cooked shrimp in each bowl with the string bean or carrot slices on top, pour the soup carefully over the shrimp, and garnish with *sansho kinomé*.

Note: In all of these recipes, you'll notice that *sansho kinomé* is used as decoration. Remember, you can replace the *sansho kinomé* with a piece of watercress or a sliver of lemon rind.

C L E A R   S O U P   V A R I A T I O N S

VARIATIONS FOR CLEAR SOUP WHICH GO ESPECIALLY WELL WITH SUSHI

1. Poached and sliced sea bream, wheat gluten bread *(fu)*, and edible chrysanthemum leaves *(shungiku).*

2. Blanched red and white steamed fishcake *(kamaboko).* Tied trefoils *(mitsuba)* for garnish.

3. Steamed fishcake *(kamaboko)*, tied trefoil *(mitsuba)*, and slivered citron or lemon peel.

4. Canned quail's eggs (pour hot water over the eggs prior to use), edible chrysanthemum leaves *(shungiku),* and wheat

gluten bread *(fu).*

5. Seaweed *(nori)*, chopped Japanese pepper plant *(sansho kinomé),* and a leaf of bamboo for garnish.

6. Bean thread sticks (mung bean threads) or Japanese yam threads *(harusamé)* cooked in boiling water until translucent,

wheat gluten bread *(fu)* with cooked and sliced green beans for garnish.

7. Diced soybean curd *(tofu)* and chives cut into 25 mm (1 in) lengths.

8. Omelette (cut into a triangular shape), wheat gluten bread *(fu)*, and cooked and thinly sliced green beans.

9. Steamed and sliced fishcake *(kamaboko)*, fresh black Japanese mushrooms *(shiitake)* or button mushrooms (cooked

in soup for 1 minute), with cooked green snowpeas for garnish.

M I S O   S O U P

There are many types of *miso,* generally the white types are 'sweet' and the red ones salty. The darker the color, the saltier the *miso.* Their textures also vary, from very smooth to chunky. *Miso* soups take only a few minutes to prepare, and a typical serving provides roughly one-sixth of the adult daily requirement of protein. Here's a recipe for just one kind of *miso* soup.

INGREDIENTS

(Serves 4)

1 liter (2½ cups) soup base *(dashi)*

8 *nameko* (or 2 *shiitake)* mushrooms, sliced

⅓ of a cake soybean curd *(tofu)*

80 ml (⅓ cup) red *miso*

4 stalks trefoil *(mitsuba)*

ground *sansho* pepper

Make the stock of your choice and assemble the supporting ingredients. *Nameko* mushrooms are available fresh and in cans; they're similar to conventional button mushrooms, but have a slippery coating. (They can be substituted with *shiitake* mushrooms.) Drain the *tofu.*

Soften the *miso* in a medium-sized bowl by adding 45 ml (3 tbsp) tepid stock and blending it with a wire whisk. If you put the *miso* directly into the stock pot, it will not be properly held in solution, and you'll find your soup is full of *miso* pellets.

Gradually ladle the softened *miso* into the stock in a medium-sized stock pot, and simmer over medium heat. (If you want satin-smooth soup, strain the soup from one pot into another.)

When all the *miso* has been added and is dissolved, add the solid ingredients. The *tofu* can be cut into 15 mm (⅝ in) cubes over the stock pot. Chop the trefoil stalks into small pieces. Keep the soup at a simmer for a few minutes until the mushrooms and tofu are heated through. Remove from heat just before it boils. Be careful not to boil the soup, as it will change the flavor.

To serve, ladle the soup into individual lacquered bowls, distributing the mushrooms, tofu, and chopped trefoil equally and attractively. Garnish with a shake or two of *sansho* pepper. Cover and serve immediately.

NOW FOR THE GOOD PART

SETTING THE TABLE

Japanese cooking is very visual. At certain imperial Japanese banquets, court etiquette demands that guests be content to merely look at their food. It's doubtful this etiquette will ever take off in the West.

A sushi chef is regarded as an artist and cooking is a highly regarded profession in Japan.

Your sushi must look good. In Japan it's not sufficient for food to simply satisfy your appetite. Texture and appearance are just as important. Things to look for are balance and harmony in size, shape, and color between the topping and rice of *nigiri-sushi* and the filling, rice, and seaweed of *maki-sushi*.

When setting the table for your meal, never lay the chopsticks flat on the table. Chopsticks are meant to rest on special chopstick rests, made of porcelain, pottery, or bamboo. Place the chopsticks in front of your guest, side by side, with both points on the rest and facing to the left. Chopsticks that point to the right are a symbol of bad luck for the Japanese. Between courses, chopsticks are always placed on the rests and it's considered ill-mannered to leave them on your plate or in your bowl.

Because tea plays such a large part in Japanese cuisine, teacups should play a large part on your table. Distinctive teacups *(yunomi)* are custom-made for sushi shops in Japan. They often carry the name of the shop and are given as presents to regular patrons.

Serving platters, bowls, chopstick rests, and teacups vary in price and style and are for sale at most Asian grocers.

If your chopsticks are joined at the top (the cheaper, disposable kind usually are), split them apart carefully nearest to the join, then:

1. Place one chopstick in the hollow between the thumb and index finger, and support it on the ring finger.

2. Hold the other chopstick with the tips of your thumb, index, and middle fingers. Manipulate the tip of the one chopstick against the tip of the other one, which is always held stationary.

3. Now pick up your roll, dip an edge gently into a little soy sauce, and convey it to your mouth.

Beginners may want to lean over their plate and keep low to the table, until they've mastered the art. And if everything goes horribly wrong and your roll disintegrates, or you drop it in your soy sauce, remember that it's quite alright to use your fingers.

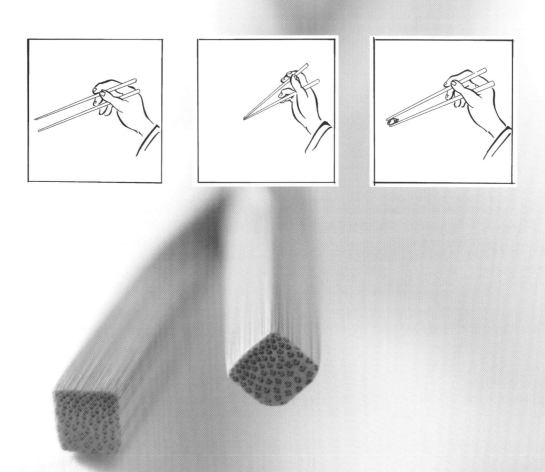

ENJOYING YOUR SUSHI

EATING WITH CHOPSTICKS

Chopsticks range in size and quality and are generally made of bamboo, willow, Hokkaido chestnut or cypress, although the finest are made from cedar, grown in Yoshino. Japanese chopsticks have pointed-ends (unlike the blunt-ended Chinese variety) so that the beautifully presented cuisine can be enjoyed with delicate precision. Eight billion sets of disposable chopsticks are used in Japan every year. *Sashimi, maki,* and even sushi can be eaten with chopsticks.

ORDER OF EATING AND PORTIONS

Sashimi, simple slices of raw fish with no rice or seaweed, is often offered as an appetizer. Placed on a small board (with a dab of *wasabi*, a small mound of *gari,* and of course an offering of soy sauce), *sashimi* gives your guests an idea of the quality of your fish. Using chopsticks, dip only the edge of your *sashimi* into the soy sauce so as not to mask the flavor of the fish. Sushi can either be served as individual portions (enough for one person), or as a large platter from which all your guests can help themselves.

INDIVIDUAL PORTIONS

For one serving, arrange *nigiri-sushi* closer to you and thin rolls *(hosomaki)* horizontally further away from you. Separate *nigiri-sushi* that has cooked toppings (omelette) from those that have raw toppings. Add one Battleship Wrap *(gunkanmaki)*. Position the thin rolls so that the seam of the seaweed faces the back. Garnish with *gari* and decorate with a bamboo leaf (if you've got in the garden). For one serving, arrange 6 to 8 *nigiri-sushi,* and one roll of *hosomaki.*

SERVING A PLATTER FOR A PARTY

It's considered ill-mannered to cram a platter with sushi, so rather use a few platters and arrange *nigiri-sushi* and rolls tastefully, with color and shape in mind. Arrange each piece of sushi in a radial pattern from the center of the platter, so guests can take pieces from any direction.

ORDER OF EATING

There is no set order in which the various kinds of *nigiri-sushi* should be enjoyed. However, in Japan, many people prefer to start off with tuna *(maguro)* and then whatever strikes their fancy. When a combination sushi plate is served, the pieces wrapped in seaweed *(nori)* should be eaten first because the crispness of *nori* doesn't last long after it's come into contact with the damp rice.

SLOWLY DOES IT

TEA

Green tea should always be enjoyed with sushi. A sip removes aftertastes and leaves your mouth fresh for the next serving. Green tea is available at all Asian grocers and should be served as your guests sit down to their meal. Their cups should also constantly be refilled, until the meal is over. Even if you're enjoying *saké* or white wine with your meal, green tea should be served. Many sushi shops use powdered green tea, rather than the more common leaf tea, because it yields the characteristic color, flavor, and aroma more quickly and is more convenient when making large quantities. Asian grocers also stock green tea tea-bags, the ultimate quick-fix.

DESSERT

Desserts are not big in Japan, but you can treat your guests to creatively cut fresh fruit. Beautifully presented slices of pineapple, banana, and orange leave the palate clean and refreshed and are the perfect ending to a healthy sushi meal.

In conclusion, one has to question whether life is indeed 'like a box of chocolates'. Or rather a selection of fat and sugar-free slim-rolled *hosomaki*.

Feeding your soul is as important as feeding your face, and evenings at home are opportunities to entertain your friends, rather than be entertained by the television.

In the wonderfully graphic pages of this book, we hope you've experienced not only the food of another culture, but some of the lifestyle: Food as art – respect for each element of the 'creation' – desserts sans dairy products – eating instruments that are far from easy to master – and of course, the addiction.

GLOSSARY
WHAT'S IN A NAME

Learning the lingo is half the fun. You have to know about ten of these words to get by, but to really raise eyebrows at a dinner party you might want to try remembering a few more. We've marked the ten must-knows with asterisks. It'll also make spotting the right ingredients on the shelves of your local Asian grocer just a little easier.

Agari:	A large cup of green tea. The term literally means 'completed'. *O-agari* is the polite form.
Agé:	A deep-fried soybean cake *(tofu)*.
Aji:	Spanish mackerel, horse mackerel.
Akami:	Flesh around the spine of tuna which is red and lean.
Anago:	Conger eel.
Anakyu:	A small, rolled sushi with cooked *anago* and sliced cucumber filling.
Aoyagi:	A variety of Japanese clam. The reddish foot portion is eaten raw.
Awabi:	Abalone.
Bakagai:	Surf clam.
Battéra:	Sushi made by pressing rice in a mold with a marinated mackerel topping.
Chó:	Triangular cross section block of tuna.
Chútoro:	Less fatty flesh from the rear block of tuna.
Daikon:	A long, white Japanese radish.
Dashi:	Japanese stock prepared with kelp and dried bonito.
Ebi:	Shrimp or prawn.
Futomaki:*	A fat, rolled sushi with different seasoned ingredients.
Fu:	High protein, wheat gluten bread which is used in soup.
Galangal:	A spice that looks similar to ginger and has a pink tinge. It can be bought fresh or sliced and bottled in brine.
Gari:*	Light pink, slightly sweet pickled ginger slices. Serve with sushi to cleanse the palate between courses.
Gesû:	Octopus – refers to the tentacles of the octopus.
Gohanmono:	Rice.
Goma:	Sesame seeds – used toasted for sushi.
Gunkanmaki:	Battleship wrap.

GLOSSARY
WHAT'S IN A NAME

Gyoku:	Rolled egg omelette *(tamagomaki)*. *Gyoku* means jewel.
Hamachi:	Young Yellowtail. Yellowtail is the common name of a number of species of amberjack – sleek migratory fish similar to tuna. The Japanese variety, *hamachi*, has light golden flesh and may display a dark streak along the edge of a fillet.
Hangiri:	Wooden rice bowl.
Harusamé:	Made from various starches and comes in fine, translucent filaments – used as an ingredient in soup.
Hikari mono:	Fish with the scales removed, leaving the skin intact with a shiny appearance.
Himo:	The stringy edge of the ark shell *(akagai)* clam.
Hirame:	Flounder. Sought-after fish used as a topping for *nigiri-sushi*.
Hosomaki:	Slender roll. *Hosomaki* is about 2.5 mm (1 in) in diameter and contains one to three ingredients plus rice. *Hosomaki* makes six bite-size rounds.
Ika:	Squid.
Ikura:	Salmon eggs (roe) – a type of Japanese caviar.
Itamaé San:	The sushi chef.
Kai:	A clam.
Kamaboko:	Fish cakes.
Kampyó:	Bottle calabash pith, which is dried in long strips.
Kani:	Crab.
Kani-ko:	Salted crabs eggs.
Kani no kamaboko:	A delicious alternative to expensive crab legs is imitation crab, which is made from pollack (a marine food-fish related to cod), potato starch, sugar, salt, coloring, and crab flavoring. It is available at most fishmongers or supermarkets.
Kappa:	Cucumber.
Katamoi:	Sea urchin.
Katsuo:	Bonito – a member of the mackerel family.
Katsuo bushi:	Dried fish shavings, which are a principle ingredient in Japanese soup.
Kazunoko:	Herring eggs.
Kinomé:	Young leaves of the prickly ash tree, used as an aromatic in soup.
Kohada:	A marinated Japanese fish, similar to a sardine, with silvery skin – used for topping on *nigiri-sushi*.
Kombu:	Kelp sea vegetable used for *dashi* preparation.
Maguro:	Tuna.

GLOSSARY
WHAT'S IN A NAME

Maki-sushi:*	Medium-sized, rolled sushi with *nori* on the outside and seasoned egg, vegetables, and fish in the center.
Masago:	Crab roe.
Matsumae-zuke:	A mixture of *saké* and soy sauce used for preserving.
Miso:*	A thick paste made from fermented and processed soy beans. Not surprisingly, it forms the base of Miso Soup.
Mitsuba:	A light-green herb added to soups and stock-based dishes just before serving to add aroma.
Murasaki:	Japanese soy sauce *(shoyu).*
Mirin:	A sweet wine, made from glutinous rice, used for cooking purposes.
Nameko:	A type of mushroom. They're similar to conventional button mushrooms, but have a slippery coating.
Namida:	A term that literally means 'tears', it refers to Japanese horseradish *(wasabi),* which often makes your eyes water.
Nami no hana:	Salt – quite romantically termed 'flowers of the waves'.
Néta:	Sushi filling.
Nigiri-sushi:*	Hand-formed, oval-shaped sushi with assorted toppings.
Nori:*	Seaweed in flat sheets.
Oboro:	White fish.
Odori-ebi:	A shrimp served live, so that it dances in front of your eyes and wiggles in your mouth. A delicacy for the true addict.
Ohyo:	Halibut.
Oshibori:	Small, moist hand towels given to guests prior to eating. Hot and steaming on cold days, and refreshingly cold on hot days.
Otémoto:	Chopsticks. These take some mastering and are used to enjoy all foods, except soup.
Otoro:	Fatty tuna.
Saba:	Mackerel.
Saibashi:	Kitchen chopsticks.
Sake:	Salmon.
Saké:*	Japanese rice wine, which is usually served warm. It has a kick not dissimilar to *wasabi.*
Sansho:	Greenish-brown ground tangy spice.
Sashimi:*	Freshly sliced raw fish fillets available from good fish markets.
Shako:	Grey-colored mantis shrimp.
Shari:	The basic vinegared, seasoned sushi rice used for preparing assorted varieties of sushi.
Shamoji:	Broad wooden paddle used to mix rice.

Shiitake:	Dried Japanese black forest mushrooms used in the preparation of sushi.
Shirumono:	The entire category of soups.
Shiso:	A fresh garden leaf, which is related to mint and tastes of a blend of mint and lemon. It is used as a garnish with sushi.
Shoga:	Root ginger.
Shoyu:	Light and flavorful Japanese soy sauce. Do not substitute Chinese or other soy sauces.
Shungiku:	Edible chrysanthemum leaves.
Su:	Japanese rice vinegar.
Sudarè:	A small bamboo place mat used for rolling certain types of sushi.
Sugata-sushi:	A small, whole fish (head and tail) topping a *nigiri-sushi*.
Suimono:	Clear Japanese soup.
Suzuko:	Fish roe.
Takenoko:	Bamboo shoots.
Tako:	Octopus.
Takuan:	Daikon radish pickled yellow.
Tamago yaki:	Sweet rolled omelette.
Tané:	Topping ingredients used for *nigiri-sushi*.
Tarako:	Cod roe.
Tekka-maki:*	Small, rolled sushi with tuna in the middle.
Temaki-sushi:	Hand-rolled sushi, either rolled in the shape of an ice cream cone or cylinder.
Teppo-maki:	Sushi rolls filled with seaweed *(nori)* and gourd shavings *(kanpyò)*.
Tezu:	Vinegared water.
Tofu:	High in protein soybean curd, found either plain or smoked.
Toro:	The oily part of tuna fillet.
Umeboshi:	These salt-cured plums are available in their natural orange color, or red when pickled. They are known to aid digestion.
Unagi:	Eel.
Uni:	Shrimp roe.
Wasabi:*	An extremely potent Japanese green horseradish that is traditionally served with sushi and *sashimi*.
Yunomi:	Large teacups without handles. Careful if the tea's hot.

RECOMMENDED FRESH FISH SUPPLIERS &

JAPANESE SPECIALITY STORES

KATAGIRI
224 EAST 59TH STREET
NEW YORK, NY 10022

NANIWA FOOD
6730 CURRAN STREET
MCLEAN, VA 22101

TREE OF LIFE
PO BOX 410
SAINT AUGUSTINE, FL 32085

**MARUWA FOODS COMPANY
OF AMERICA**
1737 POST STREET
SAN FRANCISCO, CA 94115

MIDORI MART LTD
2104 CHESTNUT STREET
PHILADELPHIA, PA 19103
WWW.MIDORIMART.COM

SATAKE USA INC.
9800 TOWNPARK DRIVE
HOUSTON, TX

MICHAEL TOSHIO CUISINE
1415 ROLLINS ROAD, SUITE 210
BURLINGAME, CA 94010
WWW.MICHAELTOSHIO.COM

UWAJIMAYA
10500 SW BEAVERTON-HILLSDALE HWY
BEAVERTON, OR 97005
WWW.UWAJIMAYA.COM

UWAJIMAYA
15555 NE 24TH AND BEL-RED ROAD
BELLEVUE, WA 98007
WWW.UWAJIMAYA.COM

SUPPLIERS OF INGREDIENTS & UTENSILS

USEFUL WEBSITES

WWW.SEAGULL-NY.COM

WWW.MRSLINSKITCHEN.COM

WWW.FBCUSA.COM

WWW.BOEKI.COM

WWW.KONNYAKU.COM

WWW.NPOSK.CO

INDEX

Page numbers in **bold** indicate photographs and illustrations

INDEX

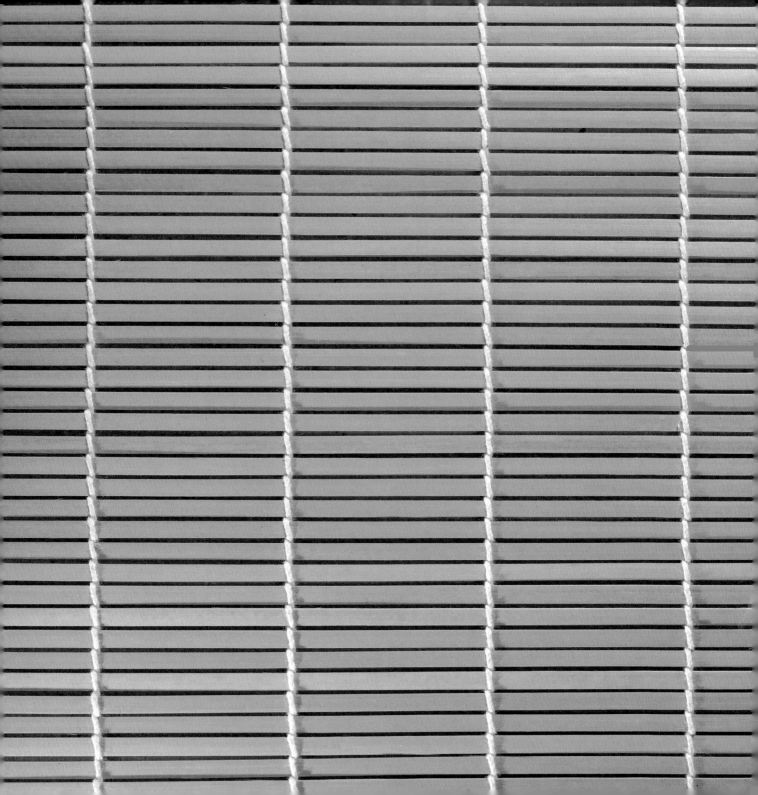